Edition Schott

Henri Vieuxtemps
1820 – 1881

Capriccio

for Viola
für Viola

opus posth.

Edited by / Herausgegeben von
Ulrich Drüner

VAB 41
ISMN M-001-10236-0

www.schott-music.com

Mainz · London · Madrid · New York · Paris · Prag · Tokyo · Toronto
© 1973 SCHOTT MUSIK INTERNATIONAL GmbH & Co. KG, Mainz · Printed in Germany

Capriccio
für Viola
aus No. 9 der op. posth.

Herausgegeben von
Ulrich Drüner

Henri Vieuxtemps

Lento, con molta espressione

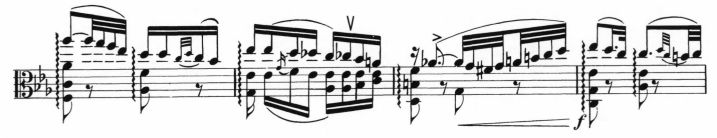

Der Originaltitel lautet: Capriccio pour Alto seul, entnommen aus: Six Morceaux pour Violon seul, suivis d'un Capriccio pour Alto seul, opus 55, No. 9 des Oeuvres posthumes. Paris, Brandus, zwischen 1881 und 1887.